INTERNET MILLIONAIRE SECRET

INTERNET MILLIONAIRE SECRET

"What Internet millionaires know you don't know"

 INTERNET MILLIONAIRE SECRET

INDEX

Let us begin...

Understanding Opportunity (Section Objectives)

Summary

Online marketing (objectives of the section)

Summary

Top 10 Reasons for Success (Section Objectives)

Summary

How to keep your most powerful resources healthy. To Yourself (Section Objectives)

A few last words (Objectives of the section)

Summary

 INTERNET MILLIONAIRE SECRET

Let us begin...

The millionaire mentality is often difficult to understand. Normal people from normal environments are going to be a great success. What makes them different from those who don't make the cut or don't achieve their goals, hopes and dreams for the future?

Observe carefully and the answers will be clear, what's more, without increasing your ability in a particular task you can get better results than the norm by simply changing the way you do them.

Let's explore the multi-million dollar mindset of the online marketer specifically over a

number of topics, and see exactly how this affects you and the way you are doing business in the most positive way.

 INTERNET MILLIONAIRE SECRET

Understanding Opportunity (Section Objectives)

- To show that to move forward, if you haven't been doing it recently, something has to change.

- To show you that no matter how idealistic it sounds, the opportunity is everywhere.

- Showing the need to understand such concepts if being successful at something is something you want to be.

INTERNET MILLIONAIRE SECRET

- Establish the basics and introduce the concept of business contacts for future reports.

- To show you that scientifically, the possibilities of achieving what you want are possible through business contacts and to show that this process is happening as we speak.

- To help explain exactly how you are in complete control of your situation, now and in the future.

- To show how your situation can change in an instant, and how you are about to make that happen on your own.

- Get out of your chair and create an opportunity with the knowledge that it will move you toward your goals quickly and effectively.

To overcome the fear of not being able to move forward, or of being too far away from your goals, make the work to achieve them seem enormous, when in reality, it is only a few steps away.

Understanding the Opportunity

Let me begin by saying that this report is totally unforeseen, it comes directly from my head, and for good reason. My goal here is to let you know a little bit about my personal thoughts related to the opportunity, how I know this is a fact, how it is presented to you, how it is detected and, most importantly, how it relates to online marketing and to you as a success. This is not a step-by-step way to do it, but it has been as important as ever to get me where I am now, and I will probably do the same for you if you can keep an open mind.

 INTERNET MILLIONAIRE SECRET

Missed Opportunities. Sound familiar?

I'll be honest; I'm not a big fan of the idea that positive thinking takes you where you want to be and that sort of thing. My way of thinking is more than that: "It's not what you know, but who you know.

Before I start thinking, let me ask you a quick question. Have you ever woken up one day and realized you missed a great opportunity the night before? Maybe it was a promotion, an opportunity to meet someone really interesting, or didn't participate in an activity you wish you had participated in?

How about a longer-term vision? Let's say you focus on something that has happened in the past that you would like to have done

differently, or someone you wish you had met when you had the opportunity, or anything related to missed opportunities.

I'm pretty sure we've all done it, including me, but have you ever wondered where you'd be if you'd gone for it and accepted the offer, or if you'd gone ahead with your idea? This is something I like to look for in the world of online business and turn my head, instead, looking at the present. All day, every day new opportunities arise, and I think it's really important that an online marketer can understand when, where and how this happens, and how to take advantage of it, what we can't do without first being able to detect the potential that arises from particular situations.

Now, I really enjoy making contacts and

creating mutual business partnerships with other marketing professionals that benefit both parties. However, I rarely see anyone making this effort consistently and in the long term, which is a shame; because we would all have exactly what we wanted if we helped each other a little more.

Let me explain. I read about a kind of scientific study (with which you may or may not be familiar) that suggests that every person in the world, no matter where they are, what country they are in, or what language they speak, is connected and knows them through a chain of seven people.

They took this type of hermit at random who lives a very lonely life in the mountains of a distant country, and chose a person in the London area to prove this.

Through research and a little juggling here and there, they managed to get from this person in London, to the other person who lives in the mountains in a distant country with his animals in seven jumps, a friend of a friend of a friend and so on. My first point here is a very important one. Whether this theory is totally correct or not, the opportunities are out there, and you should take a little time to see this, and you will immediately realize that they are not as far away as you might think, no matter how desperate the situation.

Let's imagine for a moment, you're an online marketer with a modest business, earning a couple of thousand dollars a month. How long will it take you to succeed? Who knows, the great contacts and deals that could catapult you right there through mutual agreement and profit could be just a conversation or two away. Your new business partner could be waiting around the corner for you and you could meet at any time.

If only I could give you one piece of advice - It would be this

This is my first point for each of the online sellers out there. If I had five minutes to talk to each person with an online business, seeking advice, this is what I would tell them. There are opportunities, all kinds of opportunities, things that you haven't even thought about.

They are everywhere and if you want to be a

great success, you have to take advantage of them every step of the way.

Don't get me wrong, I'm not saying you'll wake up tomorrow with an email in your inbox that will respond to all your problems, but seriously, solutions and new partnerships are ready to be taken, which brings me to the next point. If you don't take them to someone else ...of the will. Don't wait for them to come to you, go out and dig them up.

That's how the big guys make things happen. They don't do things alone, they make their contacts and help each other, whether in an intentional or purely circumstantial meeting, a large group of people makes sure that each one of them succeeds. Take ten salespeople, for example. Each one has ten times more promotional power, ten times more chances to find new contacts to increase their chances, ten times more income, and so on. You have to be able to see the power of this.

Look at it this way. Imagine that the room you're sitting in is painted pure white from top to bottom, with floors and everything. Now take a thin pen and draw a small black dot on its wall. This is you. Now take a red pen and put a little dot on top of you for each of your friends, then a blue pen for each of your friends, friends.

Imagine this process repeating over and over again, until your wall is full. See all those dots? Each one is an opportunity, each one a different person from a different lifestyle, from which you have the opportunity to meet, learn and become a mutual success.

Whether they give you a new perspective on things, or give you a little useful advice, or make you your long-term business partner, whatever it is, it's there, its closer than you think and it's waiting for someone to take it and take it to the next level, and at the same time it becomes a success. If it's not you, it's someone else.

Yours to take.

To each of these people you have something to offer, as they certainly have something to offer you. Don't get me wrong, I'm not suggesting that you go out and make friends with the whole world population, but I really want to make it clear that these opportunities are there, and that they are ready for you to take them the way you want.

This is the most important thing I think I can show you. If you see something you like, don't sit down and say, "Oh, that's great, jump in and grab it with both hands. It's yours to take right now. Don't doubt it.

Prove it works. One of the examples out of the pile

One more little analogy and I'll tell you a little story about how this site came about, and most likely many other sites and businesses before and after it. Imagine you're walking around an island in a crowded mall. Who was that person you brushed your arms with? Was it the guy who is going to tell his friends about your business and what you do, which leads to five new customers? Is this the woman who is going to give you a free beauty consultation in the future? is this the guy who is going to tell your friend about your business, and is going to hook you up with a massive marketing campaign to your list?

Stop doing it on your own for immediate results.

The potential here is totally huge. Wait, however, there is one very important thing you should know about this process of making connections, and that is that it is give and take. In a business sense, it is likely that you are giving them something and they are giving you something valuable in return.

This type of business has been around for a

long time. All we are seeing are operations that are mutually beneficial to each other. One thing I'd like to say before we go any further is that I'm talking in a purely commercial sense. I don't seriously see everyone I know as a new money-making machine, and I don't advise anyone to do that either.

All I'm suggesting here, with these black-and-white examples, is that the opportunity is out there if you're willing to take it and the results can be enormous.

We'll talk a little later about how to make contacts, and the real methods of doing it, simply because I think it's the path to total success in whatever you're trying to do. Even if it looks like you're getting a short-term pay cut. Stop trying to do things on your own

INTERNET MILLIONAIRE SECRET

and you will see the results of a team effort, in the long, medium and short term, both in terms of benefits and in terms of advantages and new opportunities opening up.

Ok, it's time for a real-world example for you, and keep in mind that this can happen to you, either in a similar situation or under totally different circumstances. How did this same product come into existence? It all started a while ago, in the year 2000, when I joined a membership website of two big name sellers. Nothing really important happened, at that time I was spending most of my working day talking to new people and trying out marketing strategies for my own membership site.

However, by simply attending some of their inquiries and participating in their community, as well as meeting these two great vendors, and several others, I also found myself in contact with great list owners and article writers. Keep in mind that I wasn't actively looking for any of this. At that time I didn't see those people as an opportunity. I was just going with the flow in reality, meeting, greeting and talking to people in the same business field as me.

Not only did I end up starting sites with two of these people, and almost starting one with another (we decided it wasn't a viable idea at the end), but three years later, here I am happily managing my e-zine and my websites, along with a call from one of them that introduces me to even more contacts. "I have this guy here, you may have heard of him, but he wants to create this site with a great sound, but I don't have time for it.

 INTERNET MILLIONAIRE SECRET

Are you ready for that?"

Sure, that sounds like a good opportunity. I left; I had a chat with this new contact, who had already been talking to the others I had met through the same site. The result? This site, 500 sales in a few weeks, each paying us $500+ for our experience and to talk to our customers first hand contacts, and some new friends and real business contacts.

Don't get me wrong, this is just an example. Forget how much and through whom and when, I'm not trying to brag here, but what I'm really doing is hammering this house. If you don't remove anything from this site other than this report, I'd love to know how many options you've opened up for yourself and will do so again in the future. As long as you have grasped this number one point, the opportunities are out there.

It is a process of giving and receiving, and always mutually beneficial.

I must also point out at this point that what I have just mentioned is an example. A single example that created more than 10 new hard contacts.

This has happened non-stop since the first contact with people in my field of expertise. Just to talk. Just by word of mouth and by not trying to do everything on my own. So let me ask you. Right now, are you working on your own? Is it open or closed to new contacts?

Next time you come up with something that sounds good to you, don't overlook it and wonder what would have happened if you had said yes. Do it, take it right away and see where it goes. Next time something comes up that sounds good to you, remember this story, and your wall painted with dots of different colors. Think about where different situations might lead you and your business and, above all, in a business environment, never expect anything in return for anything.

A kind of mutual forgotten rule, you scratch my back, I'll scratch yours.

Remember also that you should not see everyone you meet as an opportunity to make bundles with more money. I'm not going to try this, but I doubt very much that it works wonders for anyone's social life.

Always on the lookout. Try it out for yourself tomorrow morning and you'll see what happens....

So when you wake up tomorrow, and every day from now on, and a new situation arises, think of yourself: Where could this take me? What new situations will arise immediately, in a year or even ten years later? It's like seeing your whole life up to this point as a big long tail, one thing led to the other, to the other, to the other, to the other, to the other, and so on. One thing I need you to understand to complete this concept is that you are in control.

Just like you drew those dots that connect your friends, and their friends' friends on the wall before. If you chose one of them, do you think you could familiarize yourself with just a few words through other friends? Yes, you could, but it's up to you to take those steps, choose where your line goes, and select who you're going to meet and, ultimately, whether you're working to succeed or not.

If you want it to happen, go and do it. As I've shown before, understanding that you have so much control, everything is in your hands and that it's your choice is the first step to understanding how you're going to move forward. This is totally relevant to your business, no matter how strange you may think this article is for an online marketing course. I need you to understand that you have total control of what you are doing and what you are going to choose to do in the future.

Always create opportunities for yourself, leave your options open and you will never get stuck in a routine, or with an unsolvable problem.

Remember, the example above is an extreme example. Your goal is not to use everyone you know. Your goal is to do business as effectively as possible.

Don't be afraid to get involved.

Start tomorrow and you'll see results.

 INTERNET MILLIONAIRE SECRET

Summary

- This section was not planned at all. I wanted to give you the essence of what is going on in my mind every day as I conduct my online marketing because, although this is not a step-by-step guide, it is imperative that you understand it before you go any further.

- One thing I want you to try to do is to keep an open mind throughout the course. Be open to new ideas and new information presented to you. This is the only way to get the best out of it and create an abundance of awesome ideas for your business.

- I myself am not a fan of positive thinking, this section is not related to that, but is based on the concept that it's not what you know, it's who you know.

- Have you ever woken up one morning and regretted missing an opportunity, or wondered why you didn't do something the night before that you had the opportunity to do? How about in the long run? Is there something in the past that you would have liked to do differently and that you might have been doing somewhere else because of that? If so, don't worry. Everyone has these missed opportunities and this section is to make sure it doesn't happen again.

- All day, every day we are presented with new opportunities, and many don't even realize what's happening. We need to wake

you up and open your eyes to this event that surrounds you right now, because ultimately it will lead to your success.

- The starting point is to understand that not everything should be done alone. I have never met anyone successful in the world of online marketing who has not done so or who at one time or another has used this tactic on their behalf. If you want to be a success, from now on, I want you to use it too.

- Sometimes you may feel that your goals, hopes and dreams are too far away for your taste and it's frustrating because it's going to take too long to achieve them. If we assume that the first step to success is to make contacts, scientifically, everything you want and might want is never more than seven steps away from you.

- An experiment I recently discovered showed a hermit living in isolated mountains in a distant country, and the challenge was to find someone from London, England, who met him using seven steps. A friend of a friend, of a friend, of a friend, and it was a success.

- Understand right now that the opportunities are out there. You need to open your mind, step back and pay attention. If you can do this, you'll begin to see when and where opportunities present themselves. Everything you want to take with you. The big business contact that could bring two or more of you mutual but massive success could be just a conversation away.

- I'm not saying you're going to wake up tomorrow with an email in your inbox solving all your problems, but the potential to solve them is there. Opportunities in all forms and forms are ripe and ready to be picked up, and if you don't, you'll miss them and someone else will take your place.

- The power of opportunity and contact is immense. Imagine that you are a budding new salesperson who has made ten contacts just by being able to see these new opportunities coming in and meet new entrepreneurs. Ten times the income for all of you, ten times the power of promotion, ten times and the success. Can you meet ten people in the rest of your life? If you answered yes, it can be a success.

- See how success is not as far away as you think. Imagine you're in a white room. Place a small dot on a wall; this dot is you. Now place a green dot next to you for the friends you have, and a blue dot for each friend you have and so on. In no time your room will be fully covered. Looking at this room full of dots, you can see how easy it is to start from the beginning, and using this little scientific technique explained above, you have more potential than you ever dreamed of.

- In the same vein, let me ask you, if you would like, could you get a presentation from your friend you've never met before? I bet you could with a few words. The same goes for marketing. All the people you want to contact in the future for a mutually successful business relationship are right there and are accessible through someone you know.

Do you see how your success is closer than it seems?

• In addition to this, to further reinforce the way you can make good use of this effect, is to control it. What did you do when you asked your friend to introduce you to another friend? You controlled who you met. How are you going to succeed in online marketing? Through the same scientific process of controlling where you want to go instead of waiting for the opportunity to come to you.

• The opportunity can come in all shapes, forms and sizes, it doesn't have to be just meeting people. Use and apply this technique, take as much as you can as often as you can, and even if you can't predict where it will take you, at the end of it, you will always have more than you started. This opportunity to detect and seize is the key to your success, plain and simple. (We'll also talk about this later, don't worry about the details for now, just understand the concept, take it and know it exists).

• When you wake up tomorrow and any situation arises, any situation, think, where could this take me if I say yes, where could it take me if I do this instead of watching TV, who could I find if I go here instead of taking an extra lie after a long night. Remember the dots of your friends that you drew on the wall?

• Where will this take you? Who knows, I don't know, you don't know, but one thing I can tell you without a doubt is that it's going to take you forward, toward your goals. Remember, you are in control here, no one else. It is in your hands and everything depends on you.

Always create options and opportunities for yourself in this way, and you will never get stuck in a routine, not to mention how you will immediately see your rapid forward movement in the direction you want to go.

- Don't be afraid of changes or new things. I need all your attention, dedication and an open mind, that's all I ask. This will only push you in the direction you want to go.

 INTERNET MILLIONAIRE SECRET

Online marketing (objectives of the section)

• In order to share the base it is necessary to know the knowledge before moving on to specific and detailed online marketing techniques.

• To induce the right mindset for success through answering three quick questions about yourself, rather than long processes of positive thinking and goal setting.

• To make sure you know exactly what you're getting into, why you're doing this, where you are now and where you want to be in the future.

- Decrease anxiety by opening your mind to do the opposite of what you've probably been doing for most of your life when it comes to setting deadlines.

- To show you what to do with the product or service ideas you get that are not feasible to complete today.

- Put on the table the two most important things you should keep in mind and take with you everything you do related to your business.

- To explain how we as online marketers are all masters of creating multiple skills even if

you don't feel that way.

- To show that it is much easier to move your business forward, and in the direction you want it to go, that many have led you to believe through other guides and scare tactics.

 INTERNET MILLIONAIRE SECRET

Online Marketing

An overview

I'd like to take some time to talk about what you're getting yourself into.

Not just what you're getting into, but what we've all gotten ourselves into: the fascinating world of online marketing.

Let me tell you, since 1999, I've seen a lot of things. I've seen people who seem to know almost everything, I've seen friends who have had amazing successes, starting from the bottom up. I've seen people succeed in achieving their dreams and goals, and I've seen people fail and simply give up, not to mention the countless methods and guidelines for success, new systems of all kinds.

Looking back, it has been a great journey with ups and downs, ups and downs, big ups and downs. When I started working in marketing, I noticed something that scared me a little bit, and it was the high failure rate. As I progressed in building my business, trying my own methods and moving up, so to speak, I began to realize things.

People were doing their business online totally blind to the fundamental defects they were creating for themselves. I began to look back at the people I had met who had left early before reaching their goals and some things began to jump out at me. So I decided that the day I write an information product, the first things I'm going to talk about are the fundamentals of business.

This is a very important section. In fact, I remember at that time saying to myself: "When I achieve it and reach my goals, if I ever write an information product, I'm going to include a report titled "Things I'd like to know before I start. All you're about to read is background information. Things you should always have in your head as you work in your business. A kind of rule that you shouldn't deviate from, but it's not necessarily practical work that you can go through right now.

Everything I have seen and learned here at various stages of my businesses 'and would like to pass directly to you before we begin to provide you with a basis for your knowledge. Real facts to keep in mind when doing business online, or even offline, if you decide to do so in the future.

The Fundamentals of Online Business

The thing about online marketing is that anyone anywhere can start their own business. You don't need a large amount of cash to put a property, and you don't need to buy stocks, or put a large sum of money for storage, and so on. This is great, but at some point along the way, you have forgotten the basics of business.

Of course I won't bore you and pass on everything I learned in college and university, because to be honest, almost none of this applies to the real world of business. What I really want to get into in this section is you. Why are you doing what you're doing, what to expect and most importantly how to do this correctly on the ground floor, because, of course, building a solid foundation is extremely important in the short term, only in terms of survival, not to mention total and absolute success.

One thing I find with online business is, people see the opportunity there to make a lot of cash, quit their jobs and live a good life.

In a way, this is true, but they forget themselves. They see the money and their eyes light up. That's why I want to talk about you, what you want, and how you plan to get it before you move on.

Why are you here?

First, why are you here? Ask yourself that question. Why have you decided to start your own business? Why online? Maybe it was the promise of some extra money, a little extra free time. Do you want to go all the way and leave your job in the future? Or maybe you have some other motivation?

This is the basis for setting goals. Why are you here? When you've answered that question, remember it. Keep it on file, up to date and well integrated in your mind. At any difficult time that comes your way or any problems that may arise with your business in the future, remember why you are here and why you are doing this and why it is worth it. The answer to this question is what is going to stimulate you and keep you going and moving up the ladder.

Some people like to create fully developed plans around their goals, but for now we'll leave it at that. Quick and easy. It's not difficult, it doesn't take time, but it's an extremely important part of your success. All you have to do is ask yourself those three questions. Why am I here? What do I want? How do I plan to get it? Basic? You may think so, but look at it this way, without this motivation, you may find yourself waking up in five years, sitting in the same chair, in the same place, in the same situation and wondering why you haven't moved forward. It's probably because you didn't set a goal, which is achieved simply by answering those three questions. Don't let this happen to you.

 INTERNET MILLIONAIRE SECRET

This is real business

Then I want to play something I still see every day, and to be honest, it makes me wonder. I want you to remember what you're doing here. You're starting or building a business. The problem I see every day is, as we mentioned earlier, that the opportunity is there for everyone, but it doesn't seem to sink in the fact that they are starting their own business.

I understand you're a little upset that someone starts a business that you didn't know you were doing, but let me explain. I'm sure you've seen those websites with links everywhere, totally disorganized, a page full of pretty colors telling you to click on one and you'll make thousands of dollars an hour, or a charming site hosted for free with ten pop-ups on each page and a nice floral border with a bright pink animated background of happy bunnies jumping around.

It's not just the design of the sites, it's the customer service, the quality of the sales letters, the quality of the product, the price, the presentation, everything, every aspect.

It really makes me think when I land on these pages. Do these guys know they're supposed to run a business? Don't hate me yet; I know it sounds very stubborn, but its roots are based on facts.

Would you buy from these sites even if the

product sounded incredibly good? Surely you wouldn't. There are too many things on my mind. I have to ask myself too many questions.

A good salesperson knows that in addition to having a good product, the concerns of any visitor to your website should be crushed as quickly as possible. All the questions you ask yourself before you buy something about the person selling you and the product itself need to be answered and answered well, or you're just going to click and move on. The main point I'm trying to make here is to fully understand what you're getting into. With the anonymity of the Internet and the people who sell products on it, you have to remember above all that you have to be professional and business at all times. If you create something and you don't feel totally comfortable with it, chances are that it won't

be up to it and it won't do you any favors, neither in terms of money, neither in terms of free time, neither in the long nor in the short term.

Here's a good example. During the planning stages, this same report that you are reading has gone through no less than six different drafts and versions because it was not good enough. It wasn't professional enough; it didn't hit the points hard enough. This site has gone through many small changes, including three designs, a full review, four versions of scripts running in the background, two different affiliate scripts and some custom jobs.

I'm not saying you have to exaggerate, but my personal belief, based on fact is that if you've made an extra effort with something, customers will notice it, and remember you, although the most important thing is that they will buy from you in the first place. Always, always keep your work professional and of the highest quality if you want to get out of the exit blocks, or it just won't happen for you.

Your personality makes you notice

Here comes the fun part. Taking the previous idea of being professional at all times, you may feel that this next point is a contradiction in terms, and that is to inject your own personality. This is really important for the success of any online business, and it sure helps to meet people and meet new contacts and form business relationships.

Professionalism is good, but on its own, it is not enough. I see this more and more, every day with the e-zines that I receive through my mail, the reports that people send me, and the sales letters of new products or services that I read daily.

As far as I'm concerned, you're reading this, and after having read the introduction so far, you have some idea of us and who we are, how we sound and that gives the course personality. You know the source of them. If we hadn't done this, you'd be reading another boring package of text that had no background or meaning.

Here's an example a little more direct for you. At this moment, and for the rest of the course, I write to you and talk to you as if I were talking to a friend, but in a professional sense. We didn't want to create a tedious experience for you, otherwise it would turn into another block of random, boring, faceless text telling you what to do, and that's the last thing we want. We would lose, and you would lose, you would get bored, you would stop reading and you would get a negative experience with our names stuck to it. It's not good; it's not good for either of us.

How much money are you going to make?

Here's something we all enjoy talking about: money. However, it's not money you're spending, but how much you're going to earn with your business.

This is something that is certainly important to everyone reading right now. Let's talk cash. I'm sure you've seen all the big sellers out there making huge amounts of cash, hundreds of thousands of dollars a year and so on. I'm also sure you've heard or heard that you've seen a lot of people struggling to make only five hundred dollars a month as well.

Too often I see too many salespeople trying to fit into the top group when they are actually in the bottom group, something like climbing a ladder, but not reaching the middle rungs. Don't worry too much.

There's a "in the middle". As much as some sales letters would like them not to believe that this is so.

INTERNET MILLIONAIRE SECRET

You have everything you need Time in the world

I know a lot of people who make between thirty and eighty thousand dollars a year. They are not super rich, but again they have a great base to work on. I mean, don't set yourself the goal of making a million dollars a year within six months. This isn't to say it can't happen, this isn't to say it can't really happen fast, but you have to stop setting time limits, because all it does is add to your frustration and anxiety of having only so many days or weeks to reach your goals.

Work to achieve it, and you will. Throw all your time limits out the window right now.

Don't try to be the richest person in the

world. Remember the first point we talked about? Why are you doing this? This is your main goal, and don't be discouraged if you're not as rich as you expected in the first few months. In short, you will win as much as you want to win if you take into account the point of professionalism in each turn. If

are one thousand a month, one thousand a week, or one thousand a day, I want to assure you now that it can be achieved and that you are not wasting time reading this, but if you are going to achieve it, you have to stop setting deadlines right now.

Why we are all special

The fourth fundamental aspect that I want to talk to you about is generally related to the online business, and not so much to the offline business. It's about our skills. You may not think so if you've been on the scene for a while, but we're special. Yes, you are. All of us are special in that we are so skilled and probably don't even notice it. Take a look at what leads us to create the medium product.

We plan the product, create a product, design and build a website and host it, create affiliate programs, payment processors. We write our own sales material, advertise our own products, and maintain our own lists, tracking, backend sales, business administration, and customer service. Whatever. We do.

It's true that you can have web designers build your graphics for you, editors write your sales material, and so on, but if you're just getting started and don't have that kind of money to spend, it's all up to you.

This is not a problem, but the only thing I want to tell you before moving on to the next sections is to keep things structured. The information overload is bad, and if you try to be the best at everything, you'll end up tired, exhausted, confused and probably not better. Don't be so hard on yourself.

This is a good example for you. My specialty is definitely not designing graphics for websites, (far from it, believe me) which is exactly why I hired someone to do this for us. It didn't cost a lot, the whole site in fact, apart from the built-in affiliate system, cost less than three hundred dollars.

The above example included the entire membership area, the login system, the graphics, and outside of the membership area, so it's not a bad deal. This is true for every skill we have and get. If you have the skill, go for it, if you have the money and you're not as good (as my design skills) hire someone.

My second point here is that it's very rare that you want something done to you and there's no one to do it for you if you can't do it yourself. Don't give up on ideas because they seem out of your reach.

Okay, one last comment to make before we get through with today. It's all worth it.

Whether you're looking for more money or

more time to spend with your family, there's a size of business, a type of business, or a way to do things that are right for you.

The previous section may have seemed a little messy and a little nervous when it came to the issues, however, if someone took my business away from me today, and told me to start over, it would be the number one things I would be happy to know this time, that weren't so apparent the last time.

If the reasoning behind this report is not immediately clear, let me explain. If you really looked at yourself, everything you want to achieve, everything you are doing, what you have done and what you will do, now I know for sure that you are 100% comfortable with your position. You know where you're going. You know in a very

general format how you're going to get there, and you also know what you're capable of.

If some things are still unclear, feel free to go over the report again, but this time asks yourself the questions and get the answers before moving on to the next one.

A filling of space that is not. Read it again if necessary, or perhaps at a later date. Everything here is a great knowledge base for your business. Want proof? Try it, and see what happens.

 INTERNET MILLIONAIRE SECRET

Summary

- It's important to understand all these ideas before you jump headlong into creating your own business. If we are going to be successful at something, we first need background information and to understand how it works.

- Online marketing is no exception. I've seen a lot of things, a lot of ups and downs. The amazing successes, the massive failures of bankruptcy, I have seen, read and indeed own masses of guides, how, and online marketing information.

- One of the main problems is that people were making their business totally blind to the fundamental flaws of what they were creating for themselves. This was easy to see by examining the people who had failed and comparing them to the people who succeeded in my journey here. That's when I decided that when I reach my goals, I'm going to write a course based on the title: Things I'd like to know before I start. This is that course.

- Today, anyone can start their own online business. All they need is an idea, and a very small amount of cash. There is no longer a need for large amounts of investment. Looking around, it is obvious to me that for this reason people forget they are running a business, and simply see it as a quick way to make some extra money. Let me tell you that you are a businessman, or a businesswoman.

 INTERNET MILLIONAIRE SECRET

Never forget that.

• No matter how much people don't like positive thinking and goal setting, you have to. Set goals at least, because this is going to be your driving move that's going to push you toward success. No goals means no motivation, no motivation means waking up in five years and wondering why you're in the same place. Similarly, not setting goals means pursuing something you want that is always growing and improving, and further away, which means that you will never achieve it. You need a fixed goal.

• Setting some goals doesn't mean thinking positively, nor is it much work. It just requires you to answer a few questions. Think about this right now. Why you are here and why are you doing what you're

doing right now? What do you want to get out of what you're doing right now? This is all that goal setting requires. Nothing boring, nothing elaborates, but it's the difference between moving forward and staying where you are right now.

• Having a hard time or a problem you don't know how to solve? It's not a problem; refer to your goal to get some motivation. Why are you here? What are you doing right now? And what do you want to get out of what you're doing right now? That's all it takes, nothing more.

• It has to sink in that you are starting or building your own business. This isn't a game; this isn't a toy, or something for you to show your friends. It's entirely your creation, and it's there for one reason and one reason only, and it's to achieve your goals and improve your life.

- Sometimes it makes me wonder if people realize what they're doing. Professionalism is a necessity at all times. I'm sure you've seen sites filled with affiliate links, fluffy pink floral edges with bright lights that talk to you about making millions overnight. It makes me wonder if these people know you have a business. Would you buy from these sites even if the product sounded like the best thing that has ever appeared on the Internet?

- It's not about site design either. It's about professionalism. You have to have this with you in everything you do. It has to be the best job you've ever done. When I say everything, I mean your marketing, your joint ventures, your sales letters, your ad copy, your tracking, your product, your affiliate system, any contact you make with your list or any other resource you may have, in fact, anything and everything you are going to do that is related to your business.

• A good salesperson knows that in addition to having a good product, to make any sale, he has to eliminate any concern from the customer's mind when it comes to his sales letters. They should be crushed as soon as possible. Without this level of professionalism, this will not happen for you. Always think of the business, always think of the business owner, and always think of one hundred and ten percent professionalism if you are seriously looking to get somewhere.

• For example, take this product. You've gone through six drafts and several planning stages over a period of time, simply because you weren't good enough when you started. It wasn't professional enough, and it didn't hit the points hard enough.

- Don't cross the line with this, otherwise you'll never get anything, but keep it with you, keep it in front of your mind at all times and you'll do well.

- Inject his personality. This may sound like a contradiction in terms of the previous advice I gave you about being professional, however, being professional on your own is not enough. If you want to stand out, if you want to be noticed and remembered, I don't want you to be afraid to put a little bit of yourself in there. After all, if you are remembered, you are trustworthy. If you are trusted, you will make a lot more sales.

- Being professional doesn't mean being boring. For example, in this report, I talk to them as if I were talking to a friend. You're getting a lot of information and a little bit of me at the same time, something you're unlikely to forget in a hurry. Keep this along with your professionalism.

- Think about your resources. How much time do you have? Do you need more? The answer is that you can devote all the time you have available, even if it's only seven hours a week to start. You can extend the work over a longer period of time. Don't throw a good idea out the window just because you can't finish it in a few days. You are not prevented from creating a cracking product just because you don't have a lot of free time or because you don't have budgetary concerns.

• Try not to get frustrated because you are not rich. There is more to being rich and broke, and in monetary terms there are many comforts in the middle stages, where you may not have reached your goals yet, but surely you are moving toward them and in a much better position compared to when you started.

• Don't worry too much about deadlines. Deadlines equate to anxiety, frustration, and will delay you. Set a goal and work toward it, and you will.

• We're all special. We don't have a massive staff base to do things for us. We write our own sales material, advertise our own products, and maintain our own lists, tracking, backend sales, business management, and customer service. Whatever. We do it.

• You'll learn a lot of skills along the way, but again, don't throw away an idea just because you don't know how to do something. There's probably someone out there you can hire for parts of the project you can't do. For example, I'm terrible at designing graphics for websites, but that doesn't mean I stopped putting sites. I learned in the beginning, and today I have someone doing this for me.

• Congratulations, because if you can now answer the three questions: What am I doing here? Why am I doing it? What do I hope to achieve?

Then you're in the best disposition to continue, we're both in the same situation for maximum efficiency and, most importantly, probably without realizing it, just to do this, in the last thirty minutes of the course, you've already started to move forward. Let's move on.

 INTERNET MILLIONAIRE SECRET

Top 10 Reasons for Success (Section Objectives)

- To discuss the main reasons for success and failure, to try to identify any of these characteristics in the way you work and to eradicate them before entering into serious promotion of your product later in this area.

- To show you that no matter how good the previous guides sounded, if you followed them, and they didn't work, they didn't tell you the whole story.

- To show that you probably know more about online marketing than you think.

- Talk about how we all spend the day and our routines as freelancers, and how a simple problem with the transition from skivvy to full control could be holding back their progress.

- To show you that there are always parts of online marketing that someone doesn't enjoy, and to give you an idea of the number one reason why this could be standing on your feet.

- To discuss previous tips and guides you may have read and what some marketers will tell you to listen to them. If you are being told a particular phrase that has become very popular lately, no matter how nice and kind they are to you, they can't help you.

- Showing you how to move forward and how not to move forward could leave you keeping the same product for years with very few benefits. In my experience a very common mistake, I also fell into this sticky trap.

 INTERNET MILLIONAIRE SECRET

Top 10 Reasons for Success

Greetings, welcome to the section where we will look at some of the reasons why some are successful and some are not. There are many reasons why this can happen. I want to talk to you about some of the most common ones, and about some of the problems that I had to overcome on my way here and that many others that I have talked to also had to overcome. Instead of being a totally negative report in which I tell you why you are not being as successful as you would like, let us look at this from another point of view. I am going to show you all the reasons I can think of why marketers are struggling so that you can detect them and actively resolve them immediately.

Many are struggling. It's a fact. Through a plethora of no-fault situations. After all, this is not something you can go to school or college for and be taught. When we start we all feel in the dark, and mistakes are made, this is a guarantee.

As you read, I would like you to concentrate on what is being said and look for examples that sound like you, or something you can do. It's nothing to be ashamed of, nothing to be annoyed or upset about, it's something only you can think about.

"Wow, that sounds like me, I'd better leave that. That's the exact effect we're looking for here, that's all.

So, without further delay, let's start analyzing some of the reasons why some marketers are more successful than others and some of the solutions if you're having a particular problem.

Are you listening? The right people?

The first one I'd like to talk to you about is your choice of shopping guide. It's true that this doesn't apply now because you've launched, but did you ever feel like someone wasn't telling the whole story with previous guides you've bought or even been given?

It's too easy to find information about online marketing, but if that information is good, proven, proven and complete it's a completely different matter. Often, when people start, they tell me that they have been reading this free e-book that was given to them, and what I am telling them contradicts what has been written, or they read about something before but were never sure how to do things. Generally, the more you spend, the better quality you get.

It's unfortunate that many marketers don't understand that they're not being told the whole story, or even that they're being told incorrect information.

Don't get me wrong, I'm not criticizing smaller products, but understand that if you want a guide that shows you all the tips and trade secrets, it sure won't cost you $25. If you have friends in the business, or someone you know who is making this mistake, tell them.

Unfortunately, trying to point someone to a high-priced product isn't always easy to do, because it sounds like a sales pitch, but I'm wandering, let's move on.

I bet you know more than you think.

Big reason number two, is that you already knew how to do everything but you didn't do the job for some reason. There are many reasons for this, but let me say that I also experienced this, until one day I bought someone else's product, which put me in their place and made me think. Hey, this guy is big and makes a lot of money, but he already knows everything he's teaching. This encouraged me quite well and turned out to be the boost I needed to get to this stage, selling multiple products over $1000 a day for several months of the year. It was a great motivator and sometimes that's just what people need to get into action again, not necessarily the knowledge itself. This is something I have taken into account with this report, and the reason we have the objectives pages and the summaries at the end of the written versions. I hope that they have done their job, that they have made you feel as if you are progressing and learning new methods and techniques that would be useful to you. I would suggest doing something similar with their products as well.

Wasting time without even knowing it

Moving on, it's amazing how much time we lose without doing anything useful, even when we seem to be. Someone pointed it out

to me four or five years ago and said hello, I have something for you to try.

The next time you do a big job, like writing a report or building a site, record how much work you do, how much you do in how long, and then report back to me in the morning. I guarantee you that I can triple the amount you did without sacrificing quality the next day.

Intrigued, I did what she said. She came back the next day and showed me how much time she was wasting doing irrelevant things. Whether it's watching the news on TV, going to get some food, talking to some friends for a few minutes, flipping through my MP3 player tracks between each song trying to find the good ones and so on.

Here's another more recent example of this. I've been working on this report now and on some software at the same time for many months. I sat for seven hours straight (something I can rarely do with the number of projects I'm currently working on) and wrote, wrote and wrote, and came out with over 60 pages, which means that if I had really sat down and concentrated on the only project I had done, I would have done over 1200 pages in just 20 days. So here's the thing. When working, try to keep a schedule, a set of goals, or at least a record of how much you are achieving and eliminate all distractions.

Don't get me wrong, I'm not calling you lazy. I know you want to move on or you wouldn't be reading this right now. Take your time

to work in your business. Sit down, eliminate

all distractions and work straight for 12 hours. Taking a look at my desk I now have my headphones on, with the playlist running, I have my keyboard, a clock and a glass of ice water. That's it, nothing more. Best of all, there are no distractions, and I work. I suggest that, at a minimum, you draw up a calendar for your working days and set yourself goals to avoid it. It's amazing how time flies and the quantity and quality of work is affected by distractions. Try it, you may find that the pace of things accelerates.

Avoiding dirty bits does this sound like you?

Then comes the 'way of thinking to avoid' the dirty parts. Have you ever been sitting there, perhaps working or reading your guides on how to accomplish something, and said to yourself, 'Hmm, you know, I don't feel like doing that', or 'This is not what I imagined doing when I started in online marketing'? Well, you wouldn't be the only one and this could be the missing piece of the puzzle for you. In general, when you start going deeper into this business it's very different from what you see on the outside. Not only that, but things can change.

Unfortunately we, as online marketers, have to take the good with the bad and move forward in spite of everything. This sometimes results in encountering something that will require you to overcome a barrier or pull something new. Usually, when I talk to people about their online marketing, the number one thing listed here is joint ventures.

Especially the first time because you're no longer dealing with a lot of lists, but on a personal level and, in fact, it can be a bit difficult to get going if you've never done it before. As I mentioned before, they don't teach you these things in college.

So here's the thing. You need to see everything you are doing in relation to your business and wonder if it is helping or hindering you.

When you find an answer, whether in this report or elsewhere, if you don't like the idea of having to do it yourself, hire someone to do it if you can, or if not, it's time to burn some bridges. Whatever you do, don't block it and put it in the back of your mind thinking that little thing you've left out won't make much difference. In my experience, everything you do is chained to something else. Leaving one out can leave you with a big void in your online marketing.

Don't put yourself on the list of the great... Are you crazy? Are you crazy?

Let's move on to the next and probably the most troubling part of this report, and it's that you may have come across a person who says 'don't listen to the big guys,' or a report written by such a person. This confuses me to this day. The usual argument is that they are only in this by themselves, so don't listen to them, listen to me instead because I am a good person. Now I don't know how many people go to make this honest, but the attacks on the gurus, as I like to call them, seem to have become a popular business proposition for some people.

Don't believe it. That's like telling you not to listen to people who are making money, but to listen to the person who is not listening to people who are making money. Strange. My reply to the hit the guru is, no, they are not in this just for themselves. If I were to publish this report and leave it in a deplorable state, and make a few hundred sales just because I can write a sales letter, I would love to see how many people come back and buy me later or promote my products. Nobody would want to be associated with me, I wouldn't have joint ventures, I wouldn't sell any products, and so on. Not just me, it's like an unwritten rule.

You do it well, or you don't do it at all.

 INTERNET MILLIONAIRE SECRET

Broken Vase Syndrome

Then, something that personally kept me from moving forward for a year or so. I had this old site up and running that was going pretty well, considering I hadn't learned much in that period. It wasn't a small site at all. I was always updating, changing, beautifying, cleaning, tidying, maintaining and so on. Meanwhile, someone I met at about the same time I started online marketing, took three sites out of the bag. I wondered how he did it. We knew each other anyway, so she gave me access to her sites and surprised me. They didn't lack content; they were solid websites full of content.

I remember one day I talked to him and he said, "Hey, you've been working on that site for a long time, haven't you? Yes, it was, I thought to myself at the time, but I missed it.

The point. There comes a time after launching a product in which you must have everything configured and working properly so you can move to a new product. Never limit yourself to one and work on it constantly for enormous periods of time. If you find yourself doing this, you are doing something wrong.

Understand that there's nothing wrong with maintaining customer service for your products, but set it up, finish it, and get promotion.

Smooth as much as possible and as best you can. This is especially true in the case of information-based products, but even with software it is necessary to automate and move forward, not leaving it totally behind, but letting it run itself for the most part. Keep an open mind, work on new products and new projects, and don't get stuck doing one thing for years while your competition has launched ten products and is making money on them, while you continue with your original site reorganizing its design or layout.

The moment I discovered this freed me up, and here I am now working on a monstrous amount of projects with more contacts, a bigger list and more knowledge in my head than I ever imagined would fit.

Unfortunately, some of the people I met in those days were not so fortunate and are still in the pre-launch of a product they created four years ago, earning no more than they earned in the first week or so. Each to his own. I suggest you keep an open mind and know when it's time to move on to bigger, better and newer things.

I worry that I can't or won't succeed.

The following is something that is no stranger to what we talked about earlier, when it comes to avoiding the dirty parts, and that is worrying about not succeeding. Now you may not be the kind of person who cares about what other people are thinking or how they will react to your products and the things you do, which is fantastic, because you will burn bridges much faster than we do, which we hate when someone doesn't like our work. That's why you'll always get the best of everything I do personally, but for those of you who are reading and who get a little nervous when you approach something

INTERNET MILLIONAIRE SECRET

new, this is for you.

The fact is, if you're in online marketing or any business that I've found so far, you'll have to burn bridges and try something new from time to time, and carry out tasks that you're not comfortable with or that you're really going to despise doing. Let me tell you, as the kind of person who likes to please everyone all the time, I understand that it's not easy when you come across things like this. I have been insulted, yelled at, rejected, denied, denied, flatly said that the things I've done are garbage, useless, don't work and so on. I have no doubt that I will get the same in the future from people who can't bother to go out and try these methods, and you know what? If you have not experienced all this yet, let me tell you now that you will.

What a way to make you feel better, huh? Well, now that you know it, and you're ready for it, you have to accept it and move on. You'll have to find your own way to get ahead and not get discouraged when something goes incredibly wrong. Whatever you do, always push to break new limits and don't let anything discourage you because what you don't see when people tell you that they earn 20,000 a month is that they're also getting this. Each and every one of them.

Whether it's from their list, a strange customer or someone having a bad day. You'll find it, so get ready to get over it now and you'll be fine. Those of you more relaxed who don't get nicked by those things, great. Keep moving.

Knowledge is really power

Next, we have the most important knowledge. Knowledge is power, after all, and without it we would all be doomed and useless in almost everything. Well, you no longer have to worry about not having the knowledge because everything is covered in this guide for this particular method, but I do want you to make sure you are using it. The whole shopping guide after guide, guide after guide, and guide after guide is getting a little out of line for some of the people I've talked to in the past. Ten, twenty, thirty or more electronic books read. They say they've read it all but hasn't yet reached their dream of making bundles of money every month.

As we have already discussed this may be for many reasons. You may have all the knowledge of the world, but it will do nothing unless you take what you have learned and put it to good use. Don't become one of those people, because it won't take you very far, and in the end you'll end up frustrated, bored and broke.

The Freebie Imam

Next we have the gift magnet. Seeing that anyone who reads this will have bought it, I very much doubt that this will apply, but I want to be sure to catch someone right here and eliminate these problems before they start.

This comes in many forms, but I want to talk about this in general and not something specific like in the other sections. So free stuff. We all like something for nothing, but there are people who cross the line looking for free offers. Free hosting, free promotion, free web design, free sales copywriting, etc. It just doesn't work. You won't get anything if you're looking for everything that's free.

Of course, compare prices if you can, but when it comes to the fundamentals of your business, your scripts, your hosting especially, don't go with the free option because the quality will suffer, and your customers will see that too, which is something we definitely want to avoid.

I very much doubt that many of you are here buying a product so I won't stop. I thought it was best to cover it just in case and for future reference.

So we quickly moved forward and hit a wall that many vendors suffer from out there.

Never on your own

This brings me to the next point and that is don't try to do everything for yourself. A big mistake that many sellers make is that they decide they want all the benefits for themselves and try to do everything on their own.

This is all very well if you want to earn a couple of thousand dollars a month maybe but if you want to overcome that you need to expand a bit. That doesn't mean you have to go around associating on each of the sites you create, but it does mean you need to think a little more about working as a team whenever possible.

Partnerships are an example and you will be dividing profits 50/50.

However, let's say, for example, that you both have the same amount of resources to get your promotion through different contacts and each of the other lists, affiliates, Jv's and customers, mix in a little of your experience and you will end up making the same amount of cash anyway if things are even dead. However, what you will get is twice as many visitors, twice as many people tracking you, and twice as many of your affiliates adding fifty percent of your total product revenue to start with. On top of that you will be pulling twice as many resources to promote in the future.

So it's important to start working as a team. Don't worry if you still don't have anyone to work with as a team. After your first products you will begin to see some contacts land on your lap that you can join later. There is another example of this and that is when people don't want to grant affiliate commissions because they don't want to lose cash. I can totally understand it if you already have a lot of resources, but when you don't have that kind of promotional power under your belt, affiliates are the way to go.

Affiliates, however, are here to stay, and will be the difference between your 1k a month and your 20k a month and more.

Remember, affiliates are making sales that

you probably wouldn't have done anyway, so there's nothing wrong with awarding them more than the profits you're earning per sale. If you have a problem doing this you're going to have to fight, so, if this really isn't something you want to do, take some time and see how much you'd be earning if you gave 60%, for example, ten affiliates doing a particular number of sales of your product in addition to your personal sales. You should start to see how much more profitable this is than trying to do it alone, which is time consuming and costly, greatly reducing your profits unless you use these resources to influence you need to make your promotion team one person into a promotion team of ten, one hundred or even more than a thousand people. It is at this stage that this point really begins to become clear.

So there it is. The main reasons why I think

they stand in the way of the objectives of marketing professionals and prevent them from succeeding. Do you see any of these in yourself? If so, remove them or fix them. No matter how you do it, just make sure you do it, because they will stop you and in all the examples above they will prevent you from succeeding unless you can overcome them.

It is a fact that we, as online marketers as I have mentioned before, have to be multi-skilled. When you enter the scene it is very, very rare and unlikely that you have everything you need to be successful, and there will be many problems, walls and obstacles that you have to overcome personally before you can make a success of this. You see, we, the marketing professionals, are all small boxes of versatility, (you included). This is the most powerful tool of all we have at our disposal and will make us all succeed. Unfortunately as good as it is for those of us who understand this, it is detrimental to those who don't understand it, and will continue to buy guide after guide, becoming frustrated and failing until or quit, or learn this.

Well, I hope you enjoyed this report. In fact, it's the most negative of all, and I prefer to focus on success rather than why people fail. Unfortunately, it had to be done and it was too important to leave it out and not count it.

We will end here now, but before we do, I just want to take note. If none of the above applies to you right now, that's great. Take advantage of the knowledge contained in this report, put it into practice and hope to see how many successful products come from you. However, be careful, just because you don't have these problems right now, you can develop any of them later. Don't forget what you just read and you will do well.

Summary

- Greetings, welcome to the section where we will discuss why some people are successful and some are not, from the main factors that led to the failures and successes of all the people I met personally along the way. That came and went, that failed and quit, that succeeded and quit their jobs and bought ridiculously large houses and expensive cars.

- There are many different reasons for success, and each one is different, but what I would like to concentrate on now are two simple questions I ask almost everyone I know when they reach the top of their marketing, be it success or failure. Why do you think you didn't? And of course, why do you think you did it? You'd be surprised at the results, I'm sure you would. Let's look at this information now.

- The first thing I'd like to talk about is your choice of buying guides.

This doesn't apply as much now, since you have this in your hands, but it's definitely something I'd like you to keep in mind in the future.

- Too often, when people are starting out, they tell me that they have been reading this free eBooks or that they have visited this free site. They've taken a lot of information out of it, and what I'm telling them to do, and what other vendors are telling them to do contradicts what they've been told wherever they've been before. The general rule is that the more you spend, the more you spend, and the better you're going to do.

• I don't deny that small courses and cheap courses can be useful, and I'm not saying that what I'm teaching you here is to be everything and finish all the information and the only way to be a success, but understand that if you want a guide that really shows you solid marketing information, someone isn't going to reveal all their best tactics for free.

• So my advice is to always look for top quality products if you want the whole story. I doubt anyone would consider selling a guide that would cost more than $500 if everything was of poor quality. It would be devastating to your business, and it's not something buyers will quickly forget. Likewise, if you have friends or make contacts that rely on small e-books for their marketing information, let them know that premium products are the way to go. Not necessarily this guide, I'm not trying to get you to sell for me, but any well-known seller with a top quality product is your best bet if you want to learn new things and serious techniques. Remember it's not hard to sell them, just point them in the right direction in a friendly way. The best thing for you is that your marketing contacts and customers are successful.

- Moving on to the second thing that I have personally seen and even experienced, which was very close to adding me to the list of those who didn't make it, and that is that you already have all the information and know-how, but you don't realize it, and therefore you don't feel comfortable putting it into action for one reason or another.

- My personal experience of this was a little shocking. I spent a little over a thousand dollars buying a product from big sellers that claimed to reveal all its secrets. Reading I found myself thinking, hey, this guy knows a lot, makes a lot of money, but I know literally everything he's telling me. I found myself adding more to his advice in my mind as I read, sort of unconsciously saying, 'Hey, you missed a bit.

- At this point I realized it was time to start moving forward and taking action. The initial learning period was over. Be aware of this because you may find that you know more than you think, and that your success may only be a matter of you diving in and confidently taking action on everything you've learned.

- In addition, the passage from worker to boss is not the easiest thing to do, a common misunderstanding, and something else that took me for a while in 2002. The way this hit me was that a friend came to me and said, 'The next time you work in your business, or do a big job, record how much time you spend doing it and how much you do, and then report it to me, and he guaranteed me that I could triple this with a simple quarter of an hour of easy work. I did what she told me, and when I came back she showed how much time I was wasting, listening to the news, browsing songs to listen to while I'm working, picking up food, talking to some friends, making calls and so on.

- So here's the thing. When you work, try to keep a schedule if that's your thing, a set of goals for the day in list format, or at least keep track of the amount of work you're doing at the workplace and eliminate distractions altogether. It sounds minor, I know, but try it and you'll see how much more you can do when you write your reports. Being lazy has nothing to do with it. It's about that transgression of being in total control. Don't let anyone ever tell you, because it's easy, because you need to get used to it.

- Looking at my desk now, I've got my headset on with a playlist running, I've got my keyboard, a clock and a glass of ice water. That's all. It's amazing how time passes and how the quality of work is affected by distractions. Eliminate them and prosper.

- Moving on from distractions the next thing I want to talk to you about is avoiding the dirty parts, a way of thinking that is in my experience affecting almost every salesperson in their first six months of hard and serious online marketing.

- Have you ever learned something new and thought to yourself, ah well, can I skip this part and do it later, or is that not how I imagined it would be? It happens to everyone, and when you have a predetermined picture of what something should be like in your head, it's hard to do something you don't fully enjoy. It's even easier to avoid things when you have total control, like with your own business.

- For example, when I started in online marketing I thought it was about publishing paid ads, creating products and getting paid. Of course it didn't work that way, and it turns out that pulling the new Board

Adventures and first contact with people is not my strong suit, while the creative side and product creation is. What if the JV's were totally ignored, or if I had edited the techniques I learned in my mind to do only the things I enjoy most? Well, personally I would have sold other people's stuff pretty quickly again.

- So the first thing I'd like you to do now is open your mind, and ask yourself, "Is there anything I've been avoiding doing because it doesn't fit into my pre-conceptions of running a business and online marketing?

- Go deeper and answer honestly, because you may already have the key you need to succeed. You may not know it because it has been placed in the back of your mind as something you don't want to do in particular, or removed from your personal knowledge base because it's something you're not prepared to do. If you find an answer to that question, put it in your mind, write it down if you have a journal, and remember it. Also, if you find something you haven't been doing or avoiding, consciously or unconsciously, after finding the answer and writing it down, keep it in mind. Your situation will not change unless you change it.

- On a personal note to you, take it from me, even if there are aspects you don't enjoy as much as others, if you face them head-on and attack them with all your might you will find that, as your business develops, your work becomes easier and easier and it is no longer so painful to fix this. My first contact in a joint venture, for example, is something I don't like, but it's no longer necessary, because people come to me. It had to be faced to get to this point and I advise you to go deeper and do the same.

It is very likely that you will surprise yourself.

- Ok, go back to something that I personally experienced and probably one of the biggest falls that I have seen around me, in the past and no doubt in the future too, and that is the attachment to a product.

- The best example I can think of is when I had this old site up and running. It's not a small site at all. Anyway, I was constantly updating, cleaning, tidying, maintaining and so on. Meanwhile, someone I had met a few months earlier had taken three sites out of the bag, and these were serious sites, full of content.

- One day he said to me, 'Hey, you've been working on that site for a long time, it must be big enough by now. It took me a while to realize why there were some of us who kept going and others who couldn't succeed, and it was simple. Now there's nothing wrong with keeping customer support up and running and updating a site from time to time, especially if it's a membership site, but there are two important things to keep in mind. First, don't get carried away by changes, beauty, addition, etc. Second, don't try to be all things to all people. If you already have satisfied customers, that's great. Your product is good, it's time to stop trying to fix it and spend that valuable time creating multiple products and developing new ideas. It's the only way to move forward and learn.

- The moment I discovered this freed me. Here I am now working on a lot of reports, sites, scripts, with a bigger list, better resources, more knowledge and experience, more promotional power, more contacts and, curiously, more free time. If you want these things too, remember, never stop developing and advancing. Keeping customer service up to date is one thing, but constantly coming back and altering your ideas is not the best way to do things. Live and learn, and move on.

- Just to give you an idea of how powerful this is on its own, here's a real life example. When I started I met two different people. One already had their own site and another joined as a member of that site and had not yet created their own products. The one with the site is today, six or seven years later, working on that same site, he still has a full-time job and although the site is massive and full of everything you could think of in his field of expertise, he hasn't made much progress. The guy who joined this site as a member created sites, created content, products, learned, went ahead, learned, went ahead, constantly pushed his limits. He told me yesterday that he has now quit his job and is earning an average of $800 per day and will double that over the course of the year. This could be the difference between your failure and your overall success.

- Let's move on to the next aspect of worrying about not succeeding.

Many people seem to develop this over time and have already decided whether they are going to succeed or not.

- Now you may not be the kind of person who cares about what other people are thinking or how they will react to your products and the things you do, which is great, because you will burn bridges much faster than we hate when someone doesn't like our work. That's why you'll always get the best of everything I do personally, but for those of you who are reading and get a little nervous when you approach something new, this is for you.

- Let's get all this out in the open right now, okay? If you follow this path, you will sometimes experience the following. You will be shouted at, you will experience things that make you feel uncomfortable (i.e., change), you will be sworn to, you will be mistreated, you will be called a liar, you will grab money, you will be rejected, you will be denied, you will be denigrated, you will be despised, you will be told that your work is sloppy, bad or not up to the standards, and that the new idea you had will never work. No matter how good your job is, this is inevitable, whether it's from those who don't understand your work, from a frustrated client, from someone who didn't like receiving an ad from you, or from someone who made his friend subscribe to your stuff. Whatever it is, whether it's your fault or not, it will happen.

- Let's make one thing clear to you. You run your business the way you want to. It's your business; you're doing the work, creating the products, buying the guides, reaping the rewards. Never, under any circumstances, let an abusive customer, a negative friend, a family member or a frustrated customer take it out on you, depress you or discourage you from trying something new. Build new bridges, listen to people's advice along the way, but be confident, be determined, and physically hack and cut your way to success if you have to. This is not despair, this is pure determination. Don't ignore the advice, but flatten any obstacles in your path, gain new ground all day every day, and you'll find that it actually takes more effort not to do it than it takes to do it.

- Finally, there is one more thing I would like to say openly about being a success. That's doing everything on your own. Something that many salespeople, who start their own business, like to do simply because it's a change from their jobs, and they have nothing else to worry about except customers. Either this or they think they'll lose on the profit side if they involve someone else in a deal.

Quite the opposite is true.

- That doesn't mean you have to go around associating on every site you create, but it does mean you have to think a little more about teamwork whenever possible.

- Associations are an example, but you will split the profits 50%.

Let's say, for example, that you both have the same amount of resources to get your promotion through different contacts and lists of each other, affiliates, JV's and customers.

Mix in a little of your experience and you'll end up making the same amount of money anyway if things are even dead. However, what you will get is twice as many visitors, twice as many people in your tracking, and twice as many of your affiliates adding fifty percent of your total product revenue to start with, and besides that you will be pulling in twice as many resources to promote in the future.

- Don't worry if you still don't have anyone

on your contact list and you start from the beginning, once you've launched your first products you'll have. Make your business teamwork.

Make each other successful by filling the gaps in your knowledge and skills with another person and allow them to do the same in return. You will be more successful than you thought possible with the product you work on and, due to increased resources, also with future products.

- That's it for this section. Some of the smaller data, but also the more important ones, all taken directly from the real experiences we have had here. Take advantage of the knowledge contained in this report, put it into practice and hope to see how many successful products come from you. But be careful. The fact that you don't have these problems right now, you can develop any of them later.

Don't forget what you just read and you will do well.

How to keep your most powerful resources healthy. To Yourself (Section Objectives)

- To view and implement preventative measures to avoid the physical nuisance or long-term damage that can be done through the general wear and tear of online businesses every day, and to take care of your most important resource of all. You.

- Examine typing technique and how it can be improved quickly and routinely to avoid long-term damage to the hands, lower arms and wrists.

- To see accessories that can help prevent long-term damage to your hands, arms, and wrists

- Study techniques and habits that can be used to avoid disruption and degradation of vision when sitting in front of a computer screen for long periods of time.

- Examine the comfort of your physical environment and prevent damage to your body over long periods of sitting.

- To take a look at what's around you, and how to use it to your advantage to prevent you from getting sick through work and other health hazards.

- Examine the basic psychological problems that can arise in the short term through running your daily business, and how to avoid them by staying fresh, focused and stress-free.

 INTERNET MILLIONAIRE SECRET

How to keep your most powerful resources healthy. Yourself

Important Note: We are not qualified physicians. These techniques have been developed through personal experience, and you should always see a doctor before performing them, or if you have doubts about your health and want more advice.

As owners of online businesses we ourselves know very well that negative effects can be caused on ourselves through what we do. Sitting in front of computer screens, sometimes for long periods of time, sitting in the same position for long periods of time, doing tens of thousands, even hundreds of thousands of keystrokes a day can wreak havoc.

Running your own business from one day to the next can have consequences when you are unprepared or don't know how to separate from your workplace at the end of the day, all of which can easily lead to anything from bone problems to sleep loss.

In this section, however strange it may be for an online marketing report, we will analyze some of those causes, and what we do regularly to eliminate or deny the harm that is being done, and we will give you some of the techniques we use personally so that you can put them into practice for yourself.

This topic seems a bit taboo for some strange reason.

As an additional note before we begin, I have to point out that we are not qualified doctors, psychologists or physicians. What you receive here is our personal experience. Before trying, consult a competent and fully qualified authority on the matter.

All right, let's get to it. What we are going to do is divide this section into small segments where we will detail a problem, the long-term effects, and what we do to make sure our bodies and minds don't go crazy and limit the damage caused by each factor. I must emphasize, go and see someone qualified before using any of these methods as they can have different effects on different people.

Number One - The first thing I'd like to talk about is your hands, arms, and wrists. We sit here writing all day for many days of the week. The constant tapping of the keys on the keyboard can be very beneficial to our health at times. If you have pain or sprains in your arms and wrists, either during or within twenty-four hours of typing, it's a sign that we need to fix things now, before they get worse or become an unsolvable problem.

(Wrist Support)

There are a couple of methods I personally use to prevent this. The first of which is a set of lightweight sports wristbands. They are not splints, but they have a very light, spongy texture. I do not wear them while writing, as they may slightly restrict movement and further worsen the problem, but I wear them for a few hours afterwards. Because of their warming effect and promoting circulation within just one week of wearing them for an hour or so a day, it stopped any small pain or moaning.

I was getting tired of writing thousands of words every day for several months. Very practical and worth checking out. Make sure your brackets are not splinted and cover the entire wrist. Also, always buy a larger size than you think you'll need. The way these things embrace your arm, it is important that they are not too tight, otherwise they may end up doing the opposite of what they are supposed to do. Likewise, don't over-tighten them.

INTERNET MILLIONAIRE SECRET

(Writing Position and Rest)

The next step is to type the position and breaks that have become fashionable lately for both the mouse and the keyboard. Unfortunately, most people use them incorrectly, possibly causing damage to their wrists and arms. If you actually check out the instructions and any refutable typing guides, or even the instructions that come with your remains, they should only be used when you are not typing. Wearing them while writing makes your wrists stretch even further, putting them under excessive stress for sometimes prolonged periods of time.

I want you to try an experiment right now. Go open a new text document, and in your normal position, write four or five lines, and pay attention to how it feels. Don't change

anything at this time, just try and observe.

When you're done with that, open a second document and write other lines, but this time, lift your wrists and hands off the keyboard and see how relaxed you feel compared to the other method. You'll probably also notice that your arms get tired unless you lift your shoulders and feel a little straighter rather than stooping, improving your posture at the same time. Try it now, see what it feels like. It might be worth repeating this for a week or so in all your work until it becomes a habit. As you can feel immediately, the tension in your wrists is drastically reduced.

(Regular breaks)

Then it's something that everyone tells you to

do, even your family and friends most likely if you see it on the computer for long periods of time, and that's to take regular breaks. When I say regular, I don't mean every four or five hours, which is as easy to do when you're wrapped up in a piece of work as I'm sure you've already noticed, but for a minute or so every twenty minutes or so. It's only three minutes per hour, but its positive effects are definitely worth it. Increase this time if you wish, there is nothing stopping you from doing this and then take an additional five minutes at the end of each hour. One thing I will say besides this, don't pull and grab, and stretch and bend your wrists when you take this break. It's supposed to take the pressure off and it's not an extra exercise. You get enough of that when you put them to work on the keyboard.

(Go to the doctor)

Finally, if you have any questions, need more information, or are having pain where there shouldn't be, see a doctor. It may seem like a lot of trouble for nothing, but what's the point of having a successful business if you're not in good health to enjoy it?

Number Two - All right, secondly, we have vision problems.

There are several ways this can take, from blurry short-term vision after long periods of staring at the screen, over-watering, or a burning sensation when getting up in the morning and any form of dizziness.

All signs are to the least discomfort, and in the worst case; problems that need to be resolved ahead of time so that no long-term damage occurs.

(Regular short breaks)

The first thing you should do to prevent this from happening is, of course, take regular breaks again! One minute every twenty, five minutes every hour, it's up to you. This is your business now. You don't have a boss who tells you to look at a screen twelve hours a day with only one or two pauses in between, even if you know it's unhealthy to do so. Find the right balance for you and stick to it. While you're doing it, concentrate on something far away for a while. I always find that if I have been involved in a lot of work and have stopped after many hours, there is some sort of short-term partial myopia after all that gaze. It's not healthy. Concentrating on something far away for a while helps gets rid of it, but taking those regular breaks and preventing it altogether is a much better option.

(Go to the doctor or optician)

Finally, if you have long-term problems, or a problem that exceeds a particular point of severity, it's time to see an optician or someone qualified to treat you.

Number Three, we have back pain or stiffness, especially in the lower back or shoulders. It is possible that this could easily be your posture and your overall comfort when you are sitting in your workplace.

A great example of this is when I moved to this place. When I came in, all there was to sit on was a wooden chair. Eager to get on with this business, before unpacking anything else, or buying new furniture, I spent a day, maybe a day and a half sitting in this chair. I'll tell you, my back hurt for days and I was glad to get back to normal. So if you're sitting in an uncomfortable chair that makes you feel as if you've slept in a strange position, it might be time to invest in a large, reclining office chair with padded seats and a high back. They don't cost much today and are worth the investment.

Add to this a good amount of walking during your rest, a good posture, aided by the position we talked about earlier when we talked about the typing technique, and you have a great combination for many days of comfortable work.

Number Four, now here's a little something I had to deal with myself, literally coming out of a standard nine-to-five year job, turning my efforts into working at home, spending many hours on the computer trying to understand all these marketing techniques you see in front of you. Making that change isn't as easy as it sounds. My friends used to say, "Hey, you're lucky.

You make more money than I'm likely to make in the jobs I'm looking for, you can work when and for as long as you want, and do what you want when you want. Of course, until they've experienced this for themselves, they don't realize it's not that easy. Even business owners who use an office can come home at the end of the day and forget about their work, but we as online sellers are different.

The computer and your work are always there, in front of you.

It's very easy to walk past the computer and discover an hour later that you've been thinking about business ideas instead of enjoying the time out you've planned. It can affect concentration and suspension, especially if equipment and business tools are in a prominent place in the house. So here's the thing. To help you disconnect at the end of the day, take that computer out of your bedroom and sleeping area if it's there. If you have a spare room, why not turn it into an office if you haven't already? It may allow you to take your computer and your stuff out

of the main house, so that when you go to relax, you're really relaxing and leaving it behind at the end of the day.

The method of tying up the lost ends and disconnecting is one that really helped me before I could take my work out of my main home, hence the reasons why we have been doing that since the beginning of the course in a habit that is formed through repetition.

Number Five, here's something amazing that I discovered just over eight months ago. Did you know that the average office space contains thirty times more bacteria than the average toilet seat? That's pretty manic, but I can see it happening. Have some food, or a drink after work, go out for a smoke, a couple of drinks around the place, some computer improvements here and there. You

 INTERNET MILLIONAIRE SECRET

know how it is.

I know that personally my computer desk sees almost every part of my life, and because of that, it gets a good solid anti-bac every night after I'm done with it. For general health reasons, it may be good to throw away a can of anti-bac spray or a pack of wipes so you can clean up quickly for the next morning; including the mouse and keyboard especially Compressed air cans for your keyboard are also a must.

You can get these from many reputable office supply stores.

Number 6, moving to leg pains. Something that can happen for several reasons. The ones I mean right now are due to poor circulation.

A numb foot, calf pains and spasms could be related to the seating arrangement. Another good reason to buy a good chair with good cushioning behind the knees. It really is a priority if we are going to keep it comfortable and all in good working order.

In addition to this, get up and go for a walk every time you take a break. In the meantime, you may be having a drink, focusing on something further away to realign your eyes if necessary. It's really beneficial. I must also say, this is very difficult to do. I'm used to talking about marketing and online business, not about what you do every day and how you live your life, so if it seems like I'm doing more than transmitting information from my research to you as an online marketer, then I apologize. That's all it is, a little useful information to keep you in top condition, leaving your mind free for your business to

be a success.

That's all. That's all there is to it. There's not going to be a summary section for healthy online marketing, because we're all as targeted as we can go with this.

Number seven, and finally, any other concerns or health problems you may have. Go see the doctor, the doctor, the psychologist, who can help you.

Problem solving is an important part of business, as is preventing harm by establishing precautionary measures. Are yours in place or are they hurting themselves as we speak? A healthy business owner equals a healthy business.

A few last words (Objectives of the section)

- Review and reiterate some of the most important points that have been raised throughout the course, namely, the most important reasons why you will be successful and the most important reasons why you will not be able to achieve your goals, and talk about how to take advantage of them.

- To discuss the right mood for business success, and show you how to use this information to emulate success and ultimately get yourself there in the shortest possible time period.

- Reiterate the importance of staying healthy. A healthy business owner means a much greater opportunity to have a healthy business.

- revisit the habit-forming exercise of taking your fifteen minutes after each work day, to show you now what you've accomplished by doing it throughout the course, where others who didn't do it will probably have failed.

- To talk more about developing your business, the time it will take, and the positive signs that you will see, and that you should have already begun to experience that show you are going in the right direction.

- Introduce other aspects of online marketing that may be useful for further learning in the future, and show you that the way we've done things is one of many methods that really work.

- To persuade you to dive head first every day.

INTERNET MILLIONAIRE SECRET

A few last words

Greetings, and welcome to a last word. This section contains what the title suggests, some final words from us, some additional tips and tricks, and several ways in which you and your business can move forward in that important direction. Go ahead.

We've covered so much on the previous pages. I'd like to congratulate you if you've come this far. Many have given up, decided it is not for them, or have simply gone and bought report after report and never acted on it, which is a shame, but there is not much we can do about it without mind control techniques. Let us forget about the others for now and concentrate on yourself.

Surprisingly or not, the first thing I want to talk to you about is moving forward.

Monitoring your success

At all times I want you to see yourself and your business. Are you moving forward? What have you achieved in the last 48 hours working in your business? If you are viewing the same page on your screen, with the same content, then it's time to start asking questions and looking for the problem.

I'm not saying you have to be super efficient all the time, we all have good days and bad days, where we will inevitably do more or less what we know we have to do, but there is this little problem of moving forward and upwards that many people seem not to be able to understand. If you read this, you have already proven that you have grasped this concept, now as simple as it sounds; it is amazing to see how people do one of three things.

3 Factors that hinder success

The first is that either they jump from guide to guide taking the knowledge but without doing anything about it, and never advancing. This was me several years ago, until I realized that I actually had all this knowledge and knew in depth and often more about a subject than the real author. It was time to start asking questions. It turns out I already had all the knowledge, but I didn't know it. Are you in the same situation? Is it time to stop reading and start acting on the basis of the knowledge you have acquired?

The second is broken vase syndrome related to being proactive or reactive. Imagine that you wake up in the morning and decide that you are going to clean the house that day. You jump out of bed, get in the shower, have breakfast and wash the dishes afterwards, clean the surfaces.

You've already improved the kitchen by cleaning surfaces and washing dishes, haven't you? It's not like that, it's just been reactive, and it's done the necessary maintenance and things have returned to the way they were when he first woke up. There is no progress, just reactive maintenance.

So you go into the corridor ready to dust, and

at the exit you break a vase, so the vacuum comes out, and you vacuum all the pieces and take the broken pieces out, and you make everything nice and clean again. After you put your things away, you realize that you cut your leg on a sharp plant outside. Never mind, go upstairs, clean and put a plaster over it, and then go back down. What have you accomplished so far? Nothing at all. This is also reactive maintenance, because there is no progress, literally it's just maintenance. It's important to distinguish between proactive and reactive, because very often you can go home after a hard day's work and you can be so tired and feel that you've done a lot and that you've made progress, when in fact all you did was take out a little maintenance.

It's the same with business. If you sit on your computer and do your maintenance, answer some emails, change the color of your site, talk to some people about what's been going on, take a look at some products, there's nothing here to move you forward. Create those products, develop those products, improve those ideas, write those sales letters, contact those JV's, gain knowledge and understanding and you'll get tired of doing it and I guarantee you'll move at such a fast pace that no one will know how you're doing. Although they are tired and say things like "Wow, I'm really tired and I haven't done much yet", now you know why and how to avoid it. Of course, maintenance is a big part of daily life and needs to be done, but learn to differentiate between the two, learn to recognize them and recognize them and you will immediately see a difference in their speed and efficiency.

Try it, and you won't be disappointed.

This brings me to the final type of person who doesn't succeed. The maintainer. Beautifying the website twelve times a year, adding packages and stuff packages to a membership site and its current market instead of creating new products and entering new markets and creating multiple sources of specialized revenue. Think of the following: Is it time for you to redesign something? Are you redesigning because your follow up tells you that your redesign will make more sales, attract more potential customers, or attract more resources? Or you're doing it because it doesn't look as good as you'd like it to. Don't get stuck in the circle of getting better without moving forward, because you may be in the same place a few years from now, just with a slightly nicer website. It's not proactive, productive or profitable at all. I know a lot of people, who have fallen into this trap, and in fact some people are still in that trap and it doesn't look like they're going to get out of it very soon. Avoid it at all costs and you will do well, move forward, move quickly, and gain valuable knowledge and first-hand experience along the way, something that no one can put a price on because it is simply so valuable.

These aspects are more important than most will discover for themselves, and if you remember that you went back to the Top Ten Reasons for Success section, the above was put there as well, simply because I can't help but push this and push this because it really is the difference between getting somewhere and not getting anywhere at all. There is no middle ground. This should be your top priority, more important than product creation, more important than making any sale, more important than building resources or any marketing method that someone can teach you.

Next, let's look at your mood. I honestly believe through my personal experience that being in the right mood to get your business moving quickly is again more important than any marketing tactics you can learn.

The best way, no doubt, is to end the day with 15 minutes of quiet reflection. It's like keeping a diary, and it helps you not only to prepare for the day ahead, but also to resolve any problems you've encountered without the need to stress about it. It will also give you a clear idea of where to go next. Practice this often and in a few days, you'll begin to see some rather positive and strange results.

Always look ahead, and take that time to look in from that window (i.e., look at yourself from outside a window to get a better perspective of what's happening in your business). It's really important for your development and the development of your business.

If you haven't already experienced it, it's about assessing your situation and your business with an open mind. Like dreaming, sleeping, helps the organization of your thoughts. You will start seeing problems and presenting solutions to them before they happen. Retrospective is a very powerful thing, and taking this important time on a daily basis allows you to prepare for future situations that may arise, which is partially retrospective, but clearer as crystal, focused and pure, at best. I haven't met anyone who isn't capable of this yet, so if you're not sure, try it and see what starts to happen in six or seven sessions, and I assure you won't be disappointed.

Just as important is the way you send your day when you're working. Remember to disconnect, not only from the Internet, but completely. This method of carrying out relaxation and reflection, looking from the outside in and then after finishing, either ten minutes, or thirty minutes later, you turn off your computer at night. You leave your workplace, turn it off and forget everything. Staying away from work is not an easy thing to do, especially if you have your computer in your room. Even working at home and passing by ten times a day is enough to provoke thoughts, which will take your mind off your daily life and some of your

important daily tasks, and sometimes even interrupt your sleep. This is definitely something we want to avoid.

Let me ask you this, have you ever been called by your husband or wife, or by a member of your family for anything? Anything, either, dinner is ready! Or, I'm ready to go now, shall we go? Or even more likely, I'm going to bed now, are you coming too? And your answer is something like that. Hold on! I'll be there in a moment; I just need to do this first.

Another example of this type of mentality that goes full speed is along with the examples above, you have to keep getting out of bed at night, or keep going out the door ready to go, start the car and go back to the computer because you forgot to do something, or you have to do something before you go. Classic.

That's why it's important to do both exercises. Observe yourself and your business, relax, look from the outside in, and when you're done, cut it out. Disconnect, turn off your computer knowing that you haven't forgotten anything, that you don't need to worry about anything and that you don't need to wake up in the middle of the night and spend hours doing something you planned to do in a few minutes. Trust me on this, I'm not giving you instructions on how to lead your life, far from it, but be careful not to get too involved all the time or the freedom and the easy progress you've made so far could evaporate. There is speed, efficiency and determination, but then there is another level of efficiency and determination in speed. The fact that you are not working in your business any longer than your body or mind can comfortably handle does not mean that you are loafing.

The following is some of what I've been a fanatic about because without realizing it, I managed to develop random back, wrist and wrist pains, and myopia in my left eye and gain about four kilos of weight (which no longer exist).

Stay healthy. Above all, above all else, stay healthy. Take note of the healthy section of the course. Get a good chair, watch your back.

Get some of those larger than you need wrist supports, write correctly, take care of your wrists, and take care of your eyes and belly.

Take regular breaks and get regular exercise, even if it means you go out to buy weights and run a little every day.

Again, I'm not trying to tell you how to live your life in any way, but it's important to me that if you're going to be successful in the future, come to me and tell me: 'Your report drove me to action and now I'm doing every month what I earned in my last job every year' and not

Your report pushed me into action and now I'm doing every month what I gained at my last job every year, but I gained a hundred pounds, developed carpal tunnel syndrome, my back hurts and I can't see much anymore. No way, not my turn. Health always comes first. It's not good to succeed if you're too sick to enjoy it.

Çurself

We've already talked about how things don't always go according to plan, when new sites are launched, when advertising campaigns are created, when people are contacted, when joint ventures are created, whatever that may be, they may become irrelevant. Fortunately this is rare, but be prepared, because if this happens you will need patience, determination and a clear, sharp mind to solve problems quickly.

If you're up at 5 in the morning wondering why you didn't go to bed when you decided (five hours ago), don't worry, you're not alone. In fact, as I write this report it's 6:20 in the morning, almost 24 hours after I started writing it, and I'm still here because the previous texts didn't meet the standard I had planned, and with the release date approaching, it's necessary to do so. Don't do this intentionally, mind, and don't make it a habit, because it is very harmful to many things, including your health, but when things don't work as planned, be prepared to have to put in more than you originally planned.

Also, if you're awake at ridiculous times and find yourself making a lot of mistakes and it's been a long day, turn it off, turn it off and walk away and continue tomorrow. There's only one need to do this on the rare occasion that something goes wrong with a site launch. Everything else can wait.

 INTERNET MILLIONAIRE SECRET

Eternal Ideas for Your Business

Keep your imagination and mind working at all times. Once you launch your first product, if you haven't already done so, you'll immediately begin to see that ideas begin to arrive automatically.

Unless you mix with your market, it's very difficult to find problem solving ideas when you don't know what the problem is in the first place.

Mix with your market. This is something we all have to do at least once a week, observing other people, seeing your products and your marketing methods, seeing how your emails get to you, and seeing your techniques, your copy, your products and so on.

This is not for any reason related to copying, we have already talked about emulation and how to do it properly, taking someone else's methods and connecting them to your products without copying any aspect of them at all. The reason for this is only to keep your mind awake and to keep it producing idea after idea after idea after idea after idea.

Here is an example of how this works. In the last week, while I was actively interested in other marketing professionals and what they are doing, listening to their lists as a research tool, as we have commented before, I have found no less than fifteen viable ideas for products and doubled that number for presentation methods. Some wild and some crazy, but they are equal ideas.

That's why it's easier to come up with ideas once you've launched your own product and started looking at other vendors and asking them why they're doing what they're doing. You are mixing with new marketing methods, creating a basis for your follow-up and new ideas, and you are experiencing the market firsthand, allowing you to face, discover, and ultimately solve problems with your products through this research, your experience, the scripts and services you use to promote your products, and the guides you read. All of them are important to you in this way because they will form the basis of your ideas. If you're not mixing with your market you won't know any of the problems, and you won't be able to solve them, and therefore you won't have any product idea.

As an additional note to this, those fifteen ideas that occurred to me is a weekly occurrence because I have been doing this since 1999. Don't worry if you don't reach that number, don't strive to reach it. Only one of your ideas can turn out to be more profitable than all my fifteen put together. In this guide you will probably find that you don't have enough time in the world to bring all of your ideas to life; you will have too many of them. So there you have it. Mix with your marketplace. It will keep your creativity flowing, form the basis of new knowledge and experience and become one of the most important aspects of your online marketing and idea creation processes.

Gradual Progress

Okay, continuing again, I must let you know that things are gradual. There's no millionaire mentality overnight. I'm not saying for a moment that it's slow; you may find yourself with a list of over ten thousand of a single product even at the beginning, a good group of contacts and a lot of affiliates.

As you go along, it can help you keep this in mind. Keep your business as a real business'. Keep creating real products and selling absolute quality to real people and you will move on. Don't get caught up in the madness and dreams of millions in days. Have secure dreams, but don't want anyone to wake up one morning and be misguided by a cowboy, or approach removed from your business by some kind of profit scheme that offers you something for nothing, or too fast. You know the statements, the ones that are too good to be true. No doubt you've heard this before, if it seems too good to be true, it probably is. Don't lose that true business mentality and remember what we are in this game. This will allow you to protect yourself, your pocketbook, achieve concentration and keep moving toward your goals and those of your business without distractions and with minimal mistakes along the way. If you can make sure you're moving forward and can see the progress every time you leave your workstation, you're on the right track and you've won half the battle.

Keep Building Those Resources - The Key to Rapid Success

Then keep building those resources, whenever you can. Each JV

Every ad you send every person you contact, every person you contact, every person who subscribes to your list, or whatever. Start thinking in terms of resources rather than sales because these are the key to your success, resources not sales. Of course resources are there to make sales, but without them there is little profit in online marketing no matter how good it may be in promotion.

This brings me back to the previous point about gradual growth. It is important that you do not underestimate what is at your disposal. Only a small number of the quality resources we have already talked about can be extremely profitable. A single joint venture can cover several products and several years, for example. Only one joint venture. A single affiliate can attract thousands of resources, only five thousand quality subscribers can be responsible for thousands per month, and that's even before we consider joint ventures and affiliates. So as you see, just because you have to build resources, and I keep telling you that it won't be instantaneous, I wouldn't be surprised if most people thought in a year or two to get where they want to be. Of course, it's gradual, business in general, as well as with building your resource, but depending on the agreements you make and how quickly and effectively you can make progress using your knowledge, it's not the multi-year job that you may be feeling a little anxious about.

An additional note to that, always keep your resources building each other. Taking each resource, separating them into categories, and using each to build another often allows you to gain many times the benefit of a single set of resources that you previously could have kept separate and that you only benefited from once.

Also remember what this does in terms of you vs. any other online marketer out there. While they are out there paying for ads over and over again and saying things like '

This online marketing game is a scam that I will never be able to make any profit' or something like that for many years to come. This is simply because they keep spending their money on things over and over and get nothing out of it but a few sales.

Using the methods you've learned here, build and multiply, and let things multiply, and before you know it, you won't be cornered to spend money on your promotion like the rest of those who don't understand this technique of resource building and multiplication.

Mistakes are good

Next up, my favorite. He makes a lot of mistakes. We like mistakes, because they teach us something every time we make them. If you're not making a mistake, it's time for you to see the way you're working. Is he clinging to the things he knows best and avoiding breaking new ground because he's worried about making mistakes?

This course is here to minimize the mistakes made when using these methods, but that doesn't mean you won't make them at all. All this information is in our heads, but we still make mistakes. Every time we do one and find the solution, it is another tool, another ally that we can add to our arsenal that we didn't have before. Make mistakes, screw up from time to time and learn something new,

 INTERNET MILLIONAIRE SECRET

but be a pioneer, be a pioneer, be imaginative and be confident.

In addition to the previous point, have you made a mistake? Excellent, learn from it, but don't let it stop you from trying something new or coming back once you've acquired more knowledge and experience.

I can't because...

Finally, but as important as everything we've discussed so far, have you ever talked to someone who really wants to do something, whether it's establish a business, or travel somewhere, or do something they don't necessarily do every day, and when you've asked them why they don't do it, they say, ``I'd like to, but...''? Often that, but it's followed by something like 'I don't know how' or 'I'll probably mess it up' or 'I don't know if it will work'. These are the best examples of how to condemn a project or an attempted failure of a project before it has been attempted and prevent all progress from being important.

If you can say with certainty that something won't work through research and tracking, that's fine, it's common sense and logical deduction using facts, but don't scare the traffickers and don't conditions yourself to be worried about biting the bullet and going for it. After all, what's there to stop you from worrying about something that doesn't work? Actually, this is not something that stops you, because it's you who controls your own mind. It's totally up to you.

Take the step. Never say I can't. Most of the time, when people say they can't, they can do it, but they have to face fear or give up something to get what they want. Go for it. What's stopping you from launching your own products using the techniques here? Is there any real reason why you can't move forward on this point?

All the best for your business!

INTERNET MILLIONAIRE SECRET

Summary

- First of all, the idea of this report, its objectives, its summaries and reviews was for you to move forward with your business.

- What once prevented you from achieving success must now be eliminated and through the methods you have been taught, you can immediately see if you are advancing or not advancing in your business.

- Keep moving at a pace. Don't get stuck, take care. Are you being proactive or reactive? Have you progressed in the last 48 hours? If you're looking at the same things you had two days ago, it's time to start

asking questions.

- Remember what we talk about when we talk about the reasons for success, these are the most important things to keep in mind, even about product creation, real marketing techniques or anything like that.

- You have to be in the right mood to succeed, those relaxation techniques, quiet time to evaluate the situation, looking from the outside in. Continue to do them and you will begin to see an extreme rate of development in your business.

- Once you have finished working through the night, perform the exercises, then disconnect and leave. Also, when it comes to health, staying up at night worrying about your business won't do you any productive favors.

- Stay healthy. I don't want anyone who reads this to go crazy, develop a lot of products and get rich if you're going to destroy your health by doing so. It's not good to be sick and succeed.

- Get ready. Sometimes you need stubborn determination when the hours are long, and things don't always go as planned.

- Keep your imagination and mind working at all times. Once you launch your first product, if you haven't already done so, you'll immediately begin to see that ideas begin to arrive automatically. Unless you mix with your market, it's very difficult to find problem solving ideas when you don't know what the problem is in the first place.

- Things are gradual. Don't expect to wake up rich one morning, we all know it doesn't work that way in real business, again, keep going, and if you can see the development and movement forward each week, you've won half the battle.

- Keep building those resources. Every time you get the opportunity, this is the key to your success. Building all five at the same time is easy when you start launching your own products. Managing even a small number of affiliates, customers, JV's, long-term customers and lists have immense power in many situations.

- Keep your resources building on each other. It is important that all of them are built together and managed correctly at all times. Keep this in mind and you will have an almost unlimited number of resources and few problems to make a snowball at an ever faster rate as you launch more products.

- Make many mistakes. This course is here to minimize this, but just like going to school or learning some new skill, without literally practicing it, it's hard to be good. Making mistakes is good. Every 'do this' and 'don't do that' tip in this course has been drawn from mistakes and successes.

- Did you make a mistake? Great, learn from it, and move on. Don't let that stop you or scare you so that you never try anything new or try again when you have more experience.

Likewise, don't let anyone scare you. The Internet is full of all kinds of people, some will inevitably take a frustrating day at you through business.

• Step forward. Never say I can't. Most of the time, when people say they can't, they can do it, but they have to face a fear or give up something to get what they want. Go for it. What's stopping you from launching your own products using the techniques here? Is there any real reason why you can't move forward on this point?

Now it's your turn.

Visit our author page on Amazon and get more MENTES LIBRES!

http://amazon.com/author/menteslibres

If you wish, you can leave a comment on this book by clicking on the following link so that we can continue to grow! Thank you very much for your purchase!

https://www.amazon.com/dp/B082NW3LHM

www.ingramcontent.com/pod-product-compliance
Lightning Source LLC
Chambersburg PA
CBHW070633220526
45466CB00001B/161